NATIONAL
GEOGRAPHIC

T0069694

Coasts

MARY TULL

PICTURE CREDITS
Cover, pages 9, 11, 13, 15, 17, 19, 21, 23, 25, 27, 29 (all border), 30–31 (background) Owaki-Kulla/Corbis; page 1 Richard Bickel/Corbis; pages 2–3 Chris Daniels/Corbis; page 4 John Henley/Corbis; pages 6–7 (background) AFLO Foto Agency; page 6 (top) Photodisc Green/Getty Images; page 6 (bottom left and right) Mark Adams/Corbis; pages 8 and 9 Michael St. Maur Sheil/Corbis; pages 10, 13 (bottom left) Royalty-Free/Corbis; page 11 Joel Sartore/National Geographic Image Collection; page 14 The Image Bank/Getty Images; page 12 Macduff Everton/Corbis; page 13 (top left) Lynda Richardson/Corbis; page 13 (middle left) Carol Havens/Corbis; pages 13 (right), 32 (bottom) Joe McDonald/Corbis; page 15 Stephanie Maze/National Geographic Image Collection; page 16 Judy Griesedieck/Corbis; page 17 Amy Toensing/National Geographic Image Collection; page 18 Robert Sisson/National Geographic Image Collection; page 19 Dinodia Photo Library; page 20 James L. Amos/Corbis; page 21 (top) James A. Sugar/Corbis; page 21 (bottom) Corbis; page 22 Eric L. Wheater/Lonely Planet Images; page 23 Peter Bennetts/Lonely Planet Images; page 24 Comnet LTD/eStock Photography/PictureQuest; page 25 Steve Brimberg/National Geographic Image Collection; page 26 Richard Olsenius/National Geographic Image Collection; page 27 (left) George F. Mobley/National Geographic Image Collection; page 27 (right) Wolfgang Kaehler/Corbis; page 28 Vince Cavataio Photography/Pacific Stock; page 29 Michael T. Sedam/Corbis; page 32 (background) Raymond Gehman/Corbis.

Produced through the worldwide resources of the National Geographic Society, John M. Fahey, Jr., President and Chief Executive Officer; Gilbert M. Grosvenor, Chairman of the Board; Nina D. Hoffman, Executive Vice President and President, Books and Education Publishing Group.

PREPARED BY NATIONAL GEOGRAPHIC SCHOOL PUBLISHING
Ericka Markman, Senior Vice President and President, Children's Books and Education Publishing Group; Steve Mico, Vice President, Editorial Director; Marianne Hiland, Executive Editor; Anita Schwartz, Project Editor; Jim Hiscott, Design Manager; Kristin Hanneman, Illustrations Manager; Diana Bourdrez, Picture Editor; Matt Wascavage, Manager of Publishing Services; Sean Philpotts, Production Manager.

MANUFACTURING AND QUALITY MANAGEMENT
Christopher A. Liedel, Chief Financial Officer; Phillip L. Schlosser, Director; Clifton M. Brown, Manager.

ART DIRECTION
Dan Banks, Project Design Company

BOOK DEVELOPMENT
Nieman Inc.

CONSULTANTS/REVIEWERS
Dr. Margit E. McGuire, School of Education, Seattle University, Seattle, Washington
James F. Marran, Social Studies Chair, Emeritus, New Trier Township High School, Winnetka, Illinois

BOOK DESIGN
Steven Curtis Design, Inc.

MAP DEVELOPMENT AND PRODUCTION
Dave Stevenson

DIAGRAM DEVELOPMENT AND PRODUCTION
Steven Wagner

Published by the National Geographic Society
Washington, D.C. 20036-4688

Product No. 4J41757

ISBN-13: 978-0-7922-4563-6
ISBN-10: 0-7922-4563-6

Printed in Canada

12
10 9 8 7 6

Cover: A lighthouse in Portland, Maine
Page 1: Fishermen in Haiti
Page 2–3: Avalon, California

Table of Contents

What Is a Coast?

The land at the edge of the sea is a **coast**. Coasts can look very different. Some have flat, smooth beaches. Others have **sand dunes**. These form when the wind blows sand into big piles. Some coasts have no beaches at all, just rocky **cliffs**.

Some coasts are straight. Others have jagged outlines. There the sea often extends into the land as a **bay**.

Coasts are places where many people work. People fish, build ships, and load and unload goods. Of course, coasts are also places where people have fun!

Se

Cliffs

Bay

Sand Dunes

Where Are the World's Coasts?

Wherever land and sea meet, there is a coast. So, all the world's land masses, from the largest to the smallest, are bordered by coasts. There are different types of coastlines. Some are long and straight. Others are jagged. Warm coasts might be lined with palm trees. Cold coasts are covered in ice and snow.

This map of the world shows most of its coasts. How far do you live from a coast?

ARCTIC OCEAN

NORTH AMERICA

Gulf of Mexico

SOUTH AMERICA

PACIFIC OCEAN

North Atlantic Drift

North
Sea

EUROPE

ASIA

Mediterranean Sea

PACIFIC
OCEAN

ATLANTIC
OCEAN

AFRICA

INDIAN
OCEAN

AUSTRALIA

N

W　　　　E

S

0　　500　　1000　1500 miles

500　1000　1500 kilometers

The sea can warm or cool a coast.

Dunluce Castle stands on
Northern Ireland's coast

The Sea Affects Coastal Climates

Climate is the usual weather in an area—how hot or cold, how wet or dry it is most of the time. The sea can have an effect on the climate of a coast.

Ireland is a country in the North Atlantic Ocean. The weather over most of Ireland is usually cool and rainy. But on Ireland's south coast, the weather is very mild. The warm climate of Ireland's south coast is caused by the North Atlantic Drift. The North Atlantic Drift is a warm **ocean current** that flows through the colder waters of the North Atlantic.

Palm trees grow near Ireland's sunny, mild south coast.

This ocean current flows near Ireland. The sea winds off the Irish coast almost always blow in the same westerly direction. When these winds pass over the North Atlantic Drift waters, they grow warm. These warm breezes give Ireland's south coast a warmer climate than it would have otherwise.

A hurricane on the Florida coast

Hurricanes Endanger Coasts

A boat blown onto land by Hurricane Andrew

Weather on a coast can be frightening. Oceans can brew up terrible storms. The most powerful storm in the Atlantic Ocean is a hurricane. A **hurricane** is a huge, circular storm with very strong winds and heavy rain. Hurricanes gather strength over the open ocean. Most never touch the land. When hurricanes do come ashore, their high winds can cause great damage to a coast. Heavy rains may cause a lot of flooding.

Every summer and fall, hurricanes develop off the Atlantic and Gulf coasts of the United States. Some come ashore with winds of 200 miles (320 kilometers) per hour! Roofs are torn from houses. Cars blow away like toys.

Weather services track hurricanes. They warn people where the storms will travel.

Grasses provide food
and shelter for animals.

Coasts Provide Habitats

Snowy egret

Raccoon

Coasts are habitats, or natural homes for different kinds of plants and animals. Salt and fresh water mix in coast areas. Sometimes, this mixing forms the type of wet grassland known as a salt marsh. Many plants and animals live in salt marshes. Mud snails and grass shrimp hide in the grasses. Fiddler crabs scamper across the mud. Birds and raccoons find lots of food in salt marshes.

Twice each day, the level of the sea rises and falls. This movement is called the tides. At high tide, the sea floods the marsh. Salt water comes from the sea. It mixes with fresh water from rivers and streams that also flow into the marsh. This water helps marsh plants grow thick. These plants provide food and shelter for animals in the marsh.

Many sea creatures begin their lives in a salt marsh. Newborn fish and shellfish find food and safety there. When they get big enough, they will leave the marsh to live in the sea.

Fiddler crab

Grass shrimp

13

Harbors provide shelter for ships.

Boats docked in
Rio de Janeiro harbor

Harbors Are Safe Places

Harbors are areas of deep water on coastlines that provide a shelter for ships and people. Mountains and hills often surround harbors and protect them from wind and waves. Ships travel on the sea from harbor to harbor. When the weather is stormy, they head for the nearest safe harbor.

The city of Rio de Janeiro is located on the coast of Brazil, a country in South America. Rio de Janeiro has one of the most beautiful harbors in the world. Lush green mountains rise around Rio's harbor like

Rio de Janeiro's harbor

protecting arms. Many ships, both large and small, come into the harbor. Some boats bring goods to trade. Others bring tourists on big cruise ships.

Taking lobsters out
of traps

Coastal People Fish for a Living

Coasts are good places for people who fish for a living. All over the world, in tiny villages and big cities, there are people who fish. They use nets, lines, traps, and other ways to harvest food from the sea.

Lobstermen buying fish for bait

Maine is in the northeastern United States. Maine has a very long coastline. Many people who live along this coast make a living catching fish and other seafood. Along Maine's shoreline, clams dig into the sand. Offshore, lobsters creep along the seafloor.

Maine is famous for its lobsters. Lobstermen put bait in lobster traps and leave them on the ocean floor. After several days, the lobstermen haul the traps aboard their boats and open them. They lift the lobsters out and measure them. If the lobsters are the right size, they can keep them to sell. If not, they must throw them back.

Ships docked in Bombay harbor

Seaports Depend on Shipping

A coastal town or city where ships come to load and unload goods is a **seaport**. A seaport needs a good harbor. It also needs good links to land transportation such as trucking and railroads.

Seaports provide jobs for many people. Some workers load and unload ships. Other workers refuel or repair ships.

Bombay (or Mumbai) is a big city on the west coast of India, a country in Asia. Bombay has a fine harbor and is India's largest and busiest seaport. Like every other country in the world, India needs to buy and sell many things. Each day, ships enter Bombay's harbor from all over the world. Some bring goods that India's people will buy. Others carry India's products to seaports around the world.

A cargo ship at an Indian port

Coast Guard officers

People Protect Coasts

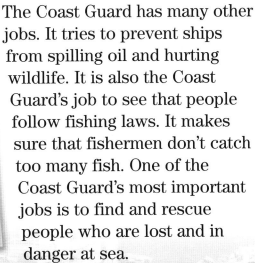
Coast Guard boat in a storm

A country's coasts are its borders. A country needs to guard its borders and see that its laws are enforced.

The United States Coast Guard protects America's coasts. Sometimes, the Coast Guard stops boats and searches them. One of the Coast Guard's jobs is to be sure that no drugs, weapons, or people are brought into the United States against its laws.

Coast Guard rescue helicopter

The Coast Guard has many other jobs. It tries to prevent ships from spilling oil and hurting wildlife. It is also the Coast Guard's job to see that people follow fishing laws. It makes sure that fishermen don't catch too many fish. One of the Coast Guard's most important jobs is to find and rescue people who are lost and in danger at sea.

Some island people live in stilt houses to stay above changing water levels.

Coastlines Can Change

Coasts are always changing. Most changes happen so slowly it is hard to notice them. But when an earthquake or hurricane hits a coastal area, big changes can happen very quickly.

Water has covered the trees that used to line this beach in Tuvalu.

Wind and water wear down a coastline. They slowly eat away at rock and sand. Over time, the sea breaks down the land. Wind and water can also build coastlines. Winds blow sand from one seashore to another. Sometimes a new beach will appear. Rivers flowing to the sea also leave behind piles of mud at their mouths.

Tuvalu is a group of tiny islands halfway between Hawaii and Australia. The sea is swallowing Tuvalu. Its coastline is shrinking. Wet marshes are replacing dry land. Salt water is seeping into the ground, so Tuvalu's people can't grow food. Their water is becoming salty, so they can't drink it. Some of Tuvalu's people have left the islands.

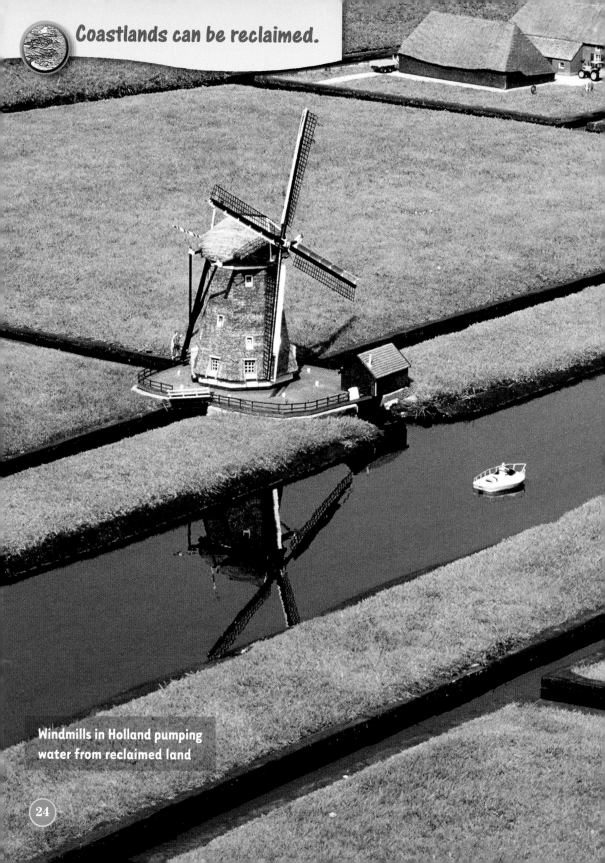

Windmills in Holland pumping water from reclaimed land

People Rebuild Coastlands

T he sea can wear away a coastline. People who live on coasts have found ways to take land back from the sea.

The Dutch people of Holland have been fighting the sea for hundreds of years. The Dutch live on the northern coast of Europe where several large rivers flow into the North Sea. Their land was mostly formed from soil carried down to the North Sea coast by these rivers. Much of this land is below sea level. Flooding from the rivers and the North Sea is a constant danger.

Long ago, the Dutch learned to hold back the sea by building seawalls called dikes. They used windmills to pump the water from the land behind the dikes. The Dutch call the areas of reclaimed land polders. Today, the pumping stations that keep the polders from flooding are powered by electricity.

Tulip farm in a polder

Some coasts are freezing.

Frozen coast on the Arctic Ocean

Arctic Coasts Are Hard to Live On

Not all coasts are warm and sunny. In the far north and the far south, in Earth's polar regions, coasts are covered in snow and ice.

The Inuit are Native American people who live in the far north, near the Arctic Ocean.

For much of the year, the Inuit live beside a frozen sea. When the water is frozen, the Inuit cut holes in the ice and drop fishing lines. Sometimes, an icebreaking ship might cut a path through the frozen sea. But it will be spring before the Inuit can use their own boats to travel.

Spring on the Arctic coast is the time Inuit families move into tents made of animal skins. They are busy while the weather is warmer. There are berries to pick and food to store for the next cold winter.

An Inuit fishing in the ice

An Inuit man in a kayak

A surfer riding a wave
in Hawaii

People Have Fun on Coasts

Beaches are one of the best places to be on a warm summer day. People build sand castles. They play in the waves and swim. Sea breezes send kites high into the air. Birdwatchers look for sea birds. Some people spend hours walking along the beach looking for shells and driftwood.

Beach towns invite people to come and enjoy the coastline. There are hotels and restaurants for visitors to enjoy. They can go horseback riding, scuba dive, or rent a bicycle built for two. Some visitors may just want to be buried in the sand. Beaches offer people all kinds of fun.

A Hawaiian beach

The Hawaiian island of Maui is a beach paradise. People come to Maui from all over the world for a tropical vacation. The sun is bright, and gentle breezes blow. Best of all, the water is warm, and the waves are high and rolling. The best surfers in the world come to Maui to test their skills. Grab your board. Surf's up!

Visual Literacy

Diagrams About Coasts

In some books, you may find information presented in diagrams. A diagram is a picture that shows how something looks. The diagram below is used on pages 4–5. It pictures land and water at a coast. Look at the diagram as you follow these steps.

How to Read a Diagram

• **Read the title.** The title of a diagram tells you what the drawing sho

• **Read the labels.** The labels tell you what the different parts of the diagram are.

• **Look at the drawing.** Think about how all of the parts of the diagram fit together.

Land and Water at a Coastline

Cliffs

Sea

Bay

Sand Dunes

Here's another diagram. What does the title tell you? What do the labels tell you?

Wildlife in a Salt Marsh

Osprey

Duck

Raccoon

Meadow Vole

Snowy Egret

Grass Shrimp

Fiddler Crab

king About the Diagrams

magine you took a trip to a ace like the one pictured in the ast diagram. Write a postcard a friend back home describing hat you saw and did.

- In the diagram above, you learn about life in the salt marsh. What special features do you think help the snowy egret find food in the marsh?

Glossary

bay a part of the sea that extends into the land

cliff a high, steep wall of rock or earth

climate the usual weather in an area

coast the land at the edge of the sea

dike a seawall that protects land from flooding

habitat a natural home for plants and animals

harbor an area of deep water on a coastline that provides a shelter for ships and people

hurricane a huge, circular storm with very strong winds and heavy rain

ocean current a flow of water through the ocean that is warmer or colder than the surrounding water

polder an area of reclaimed la in Holland

salt marsh a wet grassland in coast areas formed by the mixi of salt and fresh water

sand dune a big pile of sand formed by wind

seaport a coastal town or city where ships come to load and unload goods

tides the daily rising and falling of the sea